Moneypenny's Big Walk

Frances Usher
Illustrated by John Eastwood

OXFORD
UNIVERSITY PRESS

Dad and Lucy were having tea with Jack and Tasha.
Moneypenny was having tea too.

"When we've washed the dishes," said Jack, "we could go for a walk by the river."

"Good, good, good," said Moneypenny. "I'll race you to the gate."

"What's that dog saying?" asked Dad.

"He says he'll sit and wait," said Lucy.

They walked along the path by the river. They saw a water rat and a kingfisher. They saw two swans with their five babies. Then Moneypenny started barking.

Some children were standing by the river throwing stones into the water.

"Stop!" shouted Tasha.

"You mustn't throw stones near the swans," said Dad. "You might hurt them."

"We're only trying to hit that log," said the children.

"Be careful, then," said Dad.

They walked on along the river until they came to a bridge.

"Look, there's Mr Potter and Mrs Goodfellow," said Jack. "What's Mr Potter doing?"

THE BIG WALK STARTS HERE NEXT SUNDAY WALK TO THE OLD MILL AND HELP THE ANIMAL HOSPITAL. GET YOUR SPONSORS NOW.

"What's a sponsor?" asked Lucy.
Mr Potter got down from the ladder.

"A sponsor is a person who promises to give some
money to a good cause if you do something," he said.

"If you come on the big walk next Sunday," said Mrs Goodfellow, "your sponsors will give some money to the Animal Hospital."

"That's great," said Tasha. "Let's all go on the big walk next Sunday."

"And me! And me!" said Moneypenny. "I shall walk fastest of all."

"What's that dog saying?" asked Dad.

"He says he'll come when you call," said Lucy.

That week, they all worked hard to find sponsors. They asked people at school, they asked people in their street, they asked people in the shops. Soon they had plenty of sponsors.

"We need to get fit," said Jack, "or we'll never
finish the big walk."

"I'm as fit as a fiddle," said Moneypenny.

"What's that dog saying?" asked Dad.

"He says he's a bit fat round the middle," said Tasha.

Every evening they walked by the river to make themselves fit. The first evening they went as far as the stile. The second evening they went as far as the island. The third evening they went as far as the boats. The fourth evening Moneypenny sat down.

"Let's do something else in the evenings," he said. "We could sit at home and play Snap."

"What's that dog saying?" asked Dad.

"He says you're a very nice chap," said Lucy.

The next evening, they were walking along the river, watching the swans and their babies, when they heard a noise. "Splash! Splish! Splosh!"

They looked across the river.

"It's those children we saw before," said Jack.
"They're throwing stones again."

"That's not allowed," said Dad.

When the children saw them looking, they threw one more stone and ran away.

"Oh no, look!" said Tasha. "They've hit one of the swans."

The biggest swan was hurt.

"What can we do?" said Lucy. "We must get help quickly. Let's phone the Animal Hospital."

The people from the Animal Hospital came very quickly. A vet called Mrs Green got out of the van.

"Now, don't worry," she said. "We know just how to help."

Mrs Green and her helper, Scott, picked up the hurt swan carefully. The other swan seemed very upset.

"It thinks we might hurt the babies," said Scott.

"Everything will be all right, I promise," said Mrs Green.

They put the swan in a special bag and took it to the van.

"Why not come with us?" said Mrs Green. "Then you can see how the swan settles in at the Animal Hospital."

So they all went off to the Animal Hospital.
Moneypenny sat in the front seat. When they got
there, Mrs Green took the swan to have an x-ray.
Scott showed them round.

He showed them all the animals that were getting better in the Animal Hospital. Then Mrs Green came back with the swan.

"Its wing isn't broken," she said. "It will soon get better if we keep it here for a few days."

They told her about the children who had thrown
stones at the swans. Mrs Green shook her head.

"Perhaps they didn't mean any harm," she said,
"but we have to stop them hurting the swans."

Sunday came at last. It was the day of the big walk. Everyone waited at the bridge for Mr Potter to tell them when to start walking.

"Get set...GO!" he shouted, and off they went.

They walked a long way, past the stile, past the
island, and past the boats.

"We'll make lots of money for the Animal Hospital,"
said Jack.

"I shall make the most," said Moneypenny.

"What's that dog saying?" asked Dad.

"He says don't boast," said Tasha.

They stopped and had a drink. Then they went on. Their legs were very tired.

"Oh good! There's the old mill at last," said Lucy.

At that moment, Moneypenny stood still and sniffed the air.

"Keep going, Moneypenny," said Jack, but Moneypenny was running back down the path. They all ran after him.

"Why is he barking at that tree?" asked Tasha.

"Oh," said Lucy, "it's those children again."

The children were up in the tree. Moneypenny barked and growled.

"Get your dog away," the children shouted, "or we'll throw a stick at him."

"Oh no, you won't," said a voice.

There stood Mrs Green and Scott.

"Come down from that tree at once," said Mrs Green, and the children came down.

"I know where you live," said Mrs Green.

She took the children home while everyone else finished the big walk.

They all walked to the old mill and everyone clapped and cheered. Then Scott went to the van and took out the swan.

"Look, he's better now," he said, "and those children won't hurt him again."

Mrs Green came back and told everyone about
the swan.

"Our Animal Hospital has made him well again,"
she said, "and you have helped us with your big
walk today."

Then they put the swan carefully in the water, and
he swam away down the river.

"Good, good, good," said Moneypenny. "Aren't I clever to get it right?"

"What's that dog saying?" asked Dad.

"He says let's go home and sleep tight," said Lucy, and she gave Moneypenny a great big hug.